IDEAS

of the

HEART

Where Relationships Lie

MELINDA EDWARDS

WORKBOOK PRESS LLC
187 E Warm Springs Rd,
Suite B285, Las Vegas, NV 89119, USA

Website: https://workbookpress.com/
Hotline: 1-888-818-4856
Email: admin@workbookpress.com

Ordering Information:
Quantity sales. Special discounts are available on quantity purchases by corporations, associations, and others. For details, contact the publisher at the address above.

ISBN-13:   978-1-965732-34-2   (Paperback Version)

REV. DATE: 05/20/2021

Table Of Contents

Introduction

The heart is an organ in which allows for many functions, but the emotions and feelings in the heart is what affects day to day life. Opportunities are given for feelings to appear within the heart as both love and despair.

Variations of events can change how one feels about love and life in one little heartbeat and can look what the mind can bombard with an array of mixed emotions. During this time, I would like to explore my own array of emotions within my heart.

Those ideas include the purpose, the heartache of domestic violence, and a chaotic life of mental illness, family relationships, hope, love, humility, and success. The poetry sets the life patterns of turmoil in relationships for me.

Dedication

♥♥♥♥♥♥♥♥♥♥♥♥♥

This is a way of acknowledging those who have helped me along the way.

My deepest appreciation to....

All those who encouraged me and helped me in prayer, project, and financial support to bring this book to completion; to my parents most especially to my wonderful husband and my magnificent children.

I want to thank also my friends and relatives; this book would not be complete without you.

Most importantly, my gratitude to the Lord and Savior Jesus for His grace and companionship during this project and the Holy Spirit's faithful guidance through this assignment.

Purpose

The purpose behind wanting to share with another book in the series is to find peace within my own chaotic world inside my own head and heart by maybe allowing others to find peace within the same circumstances I have endured.

I do understand that by looking back into the past can create a series of upsetting memories, but also as a way to heal. I did not choose to be abused physically, emotionally, mentally, or sexually. I did in fact choose to run away from home, become pregnant at a young age, and get involved with drugs and alcohol. I did in fact choose to get pregnant on six different occasions in which I had four that were out of wedlock.

I ultimately had the decision to terminate one pregnancy as it was my body, but was given an ultimatum. I have had to learn skills and lifelong lessons as a result of poor decision making skills and impulsive tendencies. I had to grow up at a faster rate and grew up with my oldest daughter as I was just sixteen when she was born.

I feel wholeheartedly I would go on to choose the destination of chaos. Becoming a young mother, I believe was my calling as I was still given an opportunity to move forward despite several setbacks.

Poetry

Argument of Acceptance

Looking into all I have done
Helping those around me
Helping those who need it most
Now!
Now I need a little bit of help
I do not like this at all
Why God?
Why would you make me need so much help?
I do not understand!
I do not want to understand!
I do not like asking for all this help!
I used to be so strong
I used to be so driven
I want so much to have my old life back
The life where I could do things on my own.

Never Going to Have the Best of Me

So many times
So many tears
Runs out of my heart
Wishing and hoping
That things were different for us
Knowing you will never be mine
I will never be yours
Showing so much affection
So many tears again
Those same tears run over
They run over with a stream of emotions
Flowing and flowing
Whisking across the rocks of fate
We come across each other
Time and time again
Coming across each other
Again and again
Wanting so much more
There is so much to offer
You will never have the chance
That same chance you always had
Knowing more and more

I am the one who can show you

The happiness you deserve

Those days

Those nights

We belong together

Too bad you will never know it

You will never know until I am gone

Sweet Surrender

Surrendering to the fact that no one will ever
No one will ever give me the chance
To truly be me I want to be all I can be
To prove everyone wrong
Throughout my life story
Wanting so much to be me
Everything I do is for you
It has never been for me
No one will ever be able to prove to me
That you would ever let me be me

Temptations

Lust and desire are those sweet temptations

Giving into these temptations can break the soul

Given the chance to change the way you feel

Giving into the temptation of that someone special

Finding the only thing they want

Is that lasting temptation of lust and desire?

No More Tears

I am here to tell you
That no more tears will be lost
No more tears will be lost for you
I am tired of hurting
You said you cared I believed you
You said you would always be there
I believed you again
No more will I cry a river of tears
For someone who wants to use me
Use me for their lust and desire or gain
No more will I be alright with this
I am tired
So tired of your lies
Therefore, there will be no more tears lost for you

Too Distant for Me

I sit back and watch from a distance at how much I truly want from you

I want you so much

Knowing it hurts to be with anyone again

Knowing where my heart lies

My heart lies in the hands of someone so close

Yet, you are too distant for me

Fellowship of Man

Following through with the fellowship of man

One finds no matter what

You will always live within the village walls

Those same walls in which will help you

No matter what

They will help you

Picking you up when you are down

Believing in the fellowship of man

Finding my Higher Power

I sit in blank room and stare

Waiting for the miracle to happen for me

I never knew it could happen for a girl like me

Never believing with such horrific things I have done

That some power greater than me could still love me

I knew all along that someone loved me

Sitting back and reminiscing of days' past

Reaching to the sky above

Letting me know

This wounded and battered soul could be saved from insanity.

Pure Bliss

Linking my heart to those around me

Letting someone into help me

Life becomes a cherished path that God has set out for me

Working towards a brighter future

One day at a time

One moment at a time

Doing things of pure bliss for me

I have deserved bliss for so many years

Never taking the chance to maintain it

Never knowing how to do it

I have only learned how to maintain my pure bliss

Too Feel Love Again

I am no longer sure if I could love again

Before I never felt love

I never knew how to feel it

Loving to get together more than anything else

After all is said and done

First impressions are all we have

Freedom of my Mind

The chains have finally been released of my mind

The thoughts have slowed down so much

No more racing

No more racing at all

I longed for so long not to race the marathon in my head it has finally stopped

I have won the race

No more sleepless nights

Sitting up wondering when will I fall asleep

So many things were up there

Wandering around in such chaos

Chaos which harbors the mind, body and soul

So much time now to rest and relax

Enjoying the newfound freedom of my mind

That one night out of the clear blue

Rags to Riches

When someone thinks of rags to riches

They often think of money or prestige

My own rags to riches has nothing to do with either

I have went from broken spirited

To being a rich woman

Who now knows how to live

I love the gain I have received

Too many people believe money is everything

Money has been nothing but a delusion

A delusion of happiness

Gaining love in my life

The love I so desired is what has made me

The one that gave me a happy rags to riches story

Powerless Over Me

I have gained so much power over me

I have gained so much power over you

At least that is what my ego believed

Manipulation is what I thought as guidance

I learned manipulation was my own powerlessness

Actions and behaviors prove amends

Not just saying something to you

You stopped believing me

I cannot control that

I cannot blame anyone for that

All I can do is change for me

No one believes in fault

I know I have been that way

Not believing in anyone

Nor anything either

I want to control so many things

I cannot control anything

For I am powerless over everything except for me

Changes

Time and time again

One transition into something more

Sometimes the changes are tolerable

Sometimes the changes are horrible

No person has a written path

The only path written is through destiny

Or is it fate

I would love to know

For the chaos is sometimes great

Good times and bad times

Those are the unwritten tests of fate

Only through understanding of something more

Can one accept changes unconditionally?

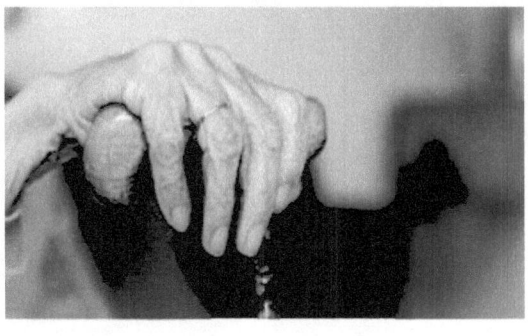

My Family Matters

Without my family

Nothing else really matters

They try to stay around

They stick around through thick and thin

When in times of desperation

When nothing else really matters most

I didn't even want to be here at one point

Someone told me my family is what matters most

When I didn't want to believe it

They showed me again that family matters most

For good times and bad times

Again no matter what

My family truly matters most to me

Freedom to be me

Sitting back in the eclipse of wanting to be me

No one would allow me to try

No one would allow me to fall

No one wanted to see me fail

I just sit back and wonder why

I want to be able to fall when I have tried

To have you there to help pick me up after the fall

Rushing in at all times before the fall

Makes me weak

It makes me oh so weak

I feel the need to prove myself

I want to prove myself to all of you

I do this

Only to have the freedom to be me

Proud

So many say that being proud

Is a sign of an enlarged ego?

So many say being proud

That you can no longer believe in anything

Nothing at all, but yourself

Being proud is finally alright

For without being proud of you

I can no longer be proud of me

Accomplishments come and go

Sometimes there is gain

Sometimes there is loss

No one can take them from you

You have earned them

Over time always maintain your idea of being proud

Reaching For My Moment

So many times I have said

I never want to find the one I want

To be with for all eternity

That is what I believed

I didn't believe I wanted anyone else

Finding true love is all anyone wants

I never believed that either

Finding that someone is hard

Keeping them is even harder

Wanting to cherish each other

To live and to learn

The things about them

The things about you

Then the things about us

Giving up is never key

For someone holds the key to your heart

Awakening

Losing faith is more difficult than living

Without faith

There is nothing left

I found that out the hard way

Rocking back and forth

Sitting up in my room

Curled up

Waiting for some sort of miracle

Never finding it before

Until the one day I was sitting there

Sitting there praying to God

Praying for help

Praying when I needed it most

For guidance for guidance to live

I mean truly live

Today was the day I felt acceptance

Today was the awakening of my life

Peace of Mind

Freeing my mind of such chaos

Creating a sense of serenity

Within the chains of chaos

Never finding that peace

No way ever giving up

Never going to take from me again

Never again are you going to take away my peace of mind

No Longer Alone

I am no longer alone

Never ever truly being alone

I have had my family

I have had my friends

Best of all I have had my God

Nothing worse than feeling alone

No longer do I feel alone

I have been reached out to

By so many

Grateful to those who care

To those who do not want to hurt me

I am grateful for no longer being alone

Forgiven

I have forgiven the ones who harmed me

Better yet

I hope the ones I have harmed can forgive me

Acting in such ways

Brings peace to the mind and soul

No longer waking up

Night after night

Watching over your shoulder

No longer wondering where someone is

That same person you harmed

Feeling the graciousness of love

Not the love of lust

I mean the love with no intentions

I mean the love which means the most

To those who care

Letter to My Children

♥♥♥♥♥♥♥♥♥♥♥♥

Mommy has been here for so long

Loving and cherishing you

Never believing that I would ever have you

Holding onto you tight

Rocking you

Night after night

Reaching to you

For the love I never felt

So many blessings happened

So many since I have been with you

You with me

Our hearts bond as one

For the love of a mother and child

Is more remarkable than any other

Loving you is all I truly feel

Loving you is all I truly need

Loving you is all I want

My children have always been my blessings in disguise

Flight of Ideas

Going from moment to moment
From time to time
Ideas fly from one place to another
Not knowing where to go
Finding myself in each of these ideas
Not knowing where to go
One moment I am quiet and content
One moment hostile and angry
Not knowing where to go with the ideas
The flight of ideas suffers inside of me
To those inside my mind
Fleeting thoughts have taken port
Taken port inside my mind
Loving every moment of peace
Despising every moment of hate
Not knowing where to go with the ideas
The flight of ideas has finally landed

Grasping My Sister Back

So many years we were best friends

For so many years we were great enemies

So many changes over time

To grasp my sister back

Never knowing along we never stopped caring

We never stopped loving each other

Come hell or high water

We have always been there for each other

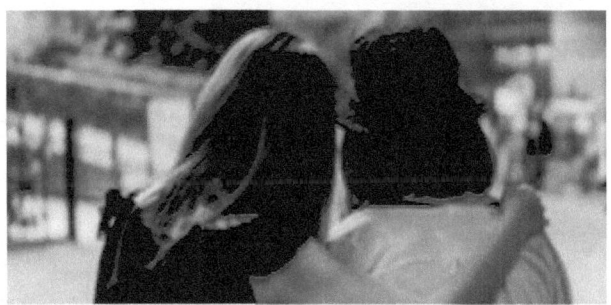

Dancing in the Moonlight

Looking under the stars

Glistening so brightly

Gazing into your gorgeous blue eyes

Turning to you so quietly

Holding you close

So close

Embracing to dance tightly under the moonlight

Feeling a sense of protection

That sense of security

So much I love to feel you close

With a refreshing sense of us

To Want My Mommy

♥♥♥♥♥♥♥♥♥♥♥♥♥

I for so long thought no one really wanted me

When I am sad All I do is sit in my room

Curled in a ball Rocking back and forth

Calling for my mommy

I am sad

Oh so sad

Wishing so much that you could hold me

I am rocking here wanting you to help me

Please help me up

Loving me is all I wanted from you

I found that I wanted you more and more

Mommy I knew you loved me all along

Brokenhearted

I have come to accept I will never be good enough for you

What makes me think I will be good enough for anyone?

I do not want to love again

The pain is too great

Too much to handle

Never gaining the freedom of having the one I love

Never wanting to open up my heart to another man

Why would you do that to another

Why would you hurt me so bad?

Then the next minute tell you

I am your friend

No!

I am afraid not

A friend doesn't hurt you

Love is supposed to be friendship

Friendship is supposed to be love

No longer is that friendship alive

No longer will keep me broken hearted

Lonely and Confused

Which way should I go

Should I go this way?

Or should I go another way

I do not know

To stay here with the one I love

Or stay with the one who was their first

Feeling the need to choose

The feeling of loneliness

The feeling of confusion in a state of chaos

I don't know which way to go

I love someone so much

I hate having to choose

That isn't fair

Why do I have to choose between you and the one I love

No longer will I be lonely and confused

I will be gone from both of you

Gone so then I don't have to choose

Waterfall of Rage

Rage is so intense for me
Flowing so fast
Then running over
Crashing so hard
Hard against the surface of my heart
You want to leave me
I want you to leave me
When will it all end
Why should I have this rage
When will you let me go
Please let me go for good
I am not what you want
You want something else so much more
All you ever wanted from is what I don't want to give
Rage of red flashes across my face
Through my veins blood boils
So hot
Then so cold
The rage against my waterfall of emotions
You make them worse
Day in and day out
Night after night
Stop playing the tears of rage against me
No longer does anyone want this
I can't handle the rage
I want so much for it to go away
Those raging waterfalls of emotions

Home

Home is where my heart tells me I should be

That place you go when you are happy

The place you go when you are sad

The simple place and time where one raises their family

A place to be proud of

When things get rough

When things are going superior

I want to be able to sit in my room

Not rocking back and forth

Living and existing in the place I call home

The place my children will be raised

The place I survive

The place I want to go home to

This is the place I want to call home

Inner Beauty

Loving me is all I need

I no longer need you to love me

I have so much to offer

Too bad you will never see it

No longer will you be able to take the best of my inner beauty

I am lovely

I know how to care

I know how to love

Too bad you will never have the chance of having this

To have someone who cares

To have unconditional love for you

I have tried to show you this

You push me away

Then bring me close

To push me away again

I can't handle the damaging effects of your emotions

You are inconsistent

I am inconsistent now

When does this stop

You never have an answer for me

I ask and I ask

The answers are never the same

Excuse after excuse

My inner beauty has been taken again

You know what

I am here to say one thing

The one thing I will have again

That no one else will take again

Is that inner beauty I have to share?

I love me so you no longer have to

Sacrifice

♥♥♥♥♥♥♥♥♥♥♥♥

Sweet sacrifice of those who have passes

Knowing where you will end

Will be so much better than where you are

Sympathy goes out to those still here

Knowing that it is hard

I mean oh so hard

To lose those in which are closest to me

Looking above for answers

Why did you take them from me?

Why do I deserve this?

I still need them here with me

To hold me when I am down

To keep me safe in the world's demise

I will always love you, grandma

You mean so much to me

Always being remembered

For the woman you are

Bleeding of Me

When I cut

I watch myself bleed

To see the hurt rush out

It never leaves though

The insanity lies inside

So strong a hold

On the past emotions

I try to talk to someone about them

No one truly cares

Why do I even bother?

I keep to myself

For I am the lost one

The hopeless one who doesn't matter

You don't want to see me get better

All you try to do is hold me down

Further and further

I fall so low

I can't get back up

The fighting is done

For I am tired

Tired of trying anymore

Heartless Soul

To those of you have seen me with some sort of emotions

Those days are long gone

I no longer want to feel anymore

For when I do

You rip the heart out of my body

The soul is the lowest you can lose

When you no longer feel anything anymore

No one can get close

No one can get close at all

No one can make me hurt anymore

I am done hurting

I will never get close to anyone again

No one will ever get through to my heartless soul

Too Much

Too much time has come and gone

Too much pain has been endured

By those outside people in my life

I know that one day I will never have to be here

I believe my time will be here soon

For I do not want to live anymore

I feel no more

When breathing doesn't even hurt

When pain inflicted doesn't hurt

The demise of my heart is all I live with

No longer caring about someone they care about

If this is unconditional love

I do not want to see conditional love

This for me is too much

The Fight is Over

So many years I have been fighting

Too many times I have tried to live

That one day at a time

That moment in time

I am here to there

I am so tired of the constant fight

That struggle in time

I have come to terms with what I am

With what I have tried to be

Nothing can change my past

I should be able to make things better

So far in life I haven't been able to that

So for me the fight is over now

First Impressions

I look to you the first time

Wondering what your intentions are

Yet, what my own intentions are

I never thought I would want to get to know you

I never knew what your first impression was of me

I will never get them anyway

No matter what

It will never be right

To the One I Love

I found you out of the clear blue

Sitting there in the grass

Working and working

I stared into those gorgeous blue eyes

Looking and gazing

Wanting so much to tell you I wanted you

I want you so badly

I felt the rush of attraction

For the first time in my life

I have finally found someone to love

Someone who has always been there for me

I long for your sweet touch

The one that protects me in your loving arms

Gazing at you

I love you so much more

You have been so close for so long

I didn't want to believe it

No not me

I thought I could never love someone else

I never thought it would happen

Until the day you walked across my path

Farmer

The hardworking man who gives his all

To the land and soil

Working hard for all of us to enjoy

Day after day I watch the farmer

Chisel the land

Dirt ridden from the land

He works the day away

Making sure we have it all

Day after day

Serenity

Laying back in the sand

Watching the waves crash

The peaceful land

Coming up along the land

Reaching my feet

Washing the soul

Reliving life

Finding the serenity of my soul

Creating a sense of peace

Within the life I live

My heart rings healthy

After such torment

I have found the serenity in me

Blessings to my Soul

While I have been watching back in my heart

The soul has been set out and brought back

Brought back to a meaning of life

That no person could do for me

Blessings to my soul

Are left to the heart and not the mind

The mind is a place of wonder

The heart lies there hoping

For the blessings to my soul

Loyalty

Becoming loyal to you is found through searching

Finding what it is you want for you

Family is loyalty

Love is a new loyalty I had never had

From someone other than cruel intentions

A cruel joke ensues when someone uses you

I am so glad to have the loyalty of my children

Also from the man I love

They have all been through trials

Tribulations have come from the struggles of loyalty

Wedded Bliss

That hot summer day

I will never forget

Being held by my pa

Headed down to the man of my dreams

Following my kids and friends of ours

Helping guide me to the altar where my life would change

I have become one with my husband

The one who has helped me during my hardest times

Has always been there through thick and thin

The good times and the bad times

My illness has taken over

He is still there by my side

I so love my wedded bliss

After saying I do that hot July day

Breeze

♥♥♥♥♥♥♥♥♥♥♥♥

Sitting out by the corn field

Enjoying the breeze of warm wind

Blowing through my long dark hair

Warming my face

Sitting in the grass by the field

Enjoying the sun

Watching the tractors breeze by

Harvesting the yields of corn

Maintaining the aroma of farm land

Watching my farmer in his tractor

Bringing in the crops

Being held in the field later

Finding passion within the field

My farmer is kindhearted

Would do anything to make me comfortable

Anytime I need

Quietly enjoying the sounds

The smells of sweet corn surround us

With a passionate kiss from my farmer

Catching Dreams

Looking through the back window

Wondering why I am going

Headed in the direction to somewhere

Looking for what I am missing

Trying to catch my dreams

All along looking past my mirrors

What I left behind

Then it appears clear of day

I found what was there along

I finally caught my dreams

Lasting Sensation

The touch along my body

His finger rolls down my side

Holding my hips

Pulling me in closely

He caresses my hair

Let's me know how I am for him

Passionately bringing my face in to him

His lips touch mine

That lasting sensation is all I need

From the man of my dreams

Seduction

Rolling down my side with his strong hand

Feeling his finger reach mine

Longing for more

Feeling his kiss upon my lips

He reaches mine

Bringing me in to a close embrace

Loving every moment

Of being close to him

Still longing for more

He continues to reach in

To ask what I want to do

I begin to cry as this is not what I truly want

You tried to seduce me

With the intentions of harm

I am scared

You are not who I thought you were

I don't even know you

Please stop

Please go

I will never feel true seduction

At peace again

You took it from me

Over and over again

Until I no longer felt safe

I no longer feel safe

Go away you cruel man

I do not want your seduction

Self-Resilience

I have become more reliable on myself

Becoming a strong woman

Who wants to be independent

Loving each thing I do on my own

Becoming stronger and stronger

I have overcome my wicked evils

Of what he took from me

I did not want that

I did not deserve what you took from me

So I came back on top

Becoming the woman, I am today

Memories

Positive or negative

Memories come and go

Life is a sail of emotions

With the memories of my babies

They have grown older

I see them become wonderful beings

Loving life

Wanting more

Seeing the world

As a beautiful memory

Awakening of the Soul

Reaching through to my inner being

I had never been so lost before

Trying to be found

I want to be grasped onto

Like a new beginning

Coming to my inner soul

I feel you grasp towards me

I feel it inside me

You have tried to help me awaken

The spirit of my soul It has become alive

Alive with you inside of me

Believe

I sit here trying to believe

That there is something more

For me to know

As if I am lost again

I believe in the Lord

As He has risen to carry me

Through some of the toughest burdens

His riches have brought me to where I am

Loving and no longer lusting for more

I am now satisfied with what I have

My life has more meaning

Then I have ever had before

Today I am glad I believe in more

www.ingramcontent.com/pod-product-compliance
Lightning Source LLC
Chambersburg PA
CBHW021654120626
46545CB00002B/853